If you want to put the George Floyd rebellion in its proper political and historical context, this is one of the works that you have to start with. The Revolutionary Meaning of the George Floyd uprising makes the unquestionable case that what we witnessed was not just a series of events aiming to reform the empire, or tamper its edges, as the bourgeois media would have us believe, but a mass movement that at its heart was and is aiming to eradicate the empire and construct a new, uncertain future. This work is a critical starting place to understand why, and further, it addresses how you can get deeper engaged. — **Kali Akuno**, co-founder, *Cooperation Jackson*

Fanon says about decolonization that in trying to change the very order of the world it is "clearly an agenda for total disorder." By this he means it is an absolute demand, unable to be mediated by policy modifications. Such a demand returns in the flames of the Third Precinct in Minneapolis, in the summer of 2020. No one has come closer than Shemon and Arturo to capturing this unfolding struggle to naming the extraordinary and contradictory character of the George Floyd Uprising — how it escapes the very history that produces it, both unique and inevitable, a true insurgency, progenitor to a hundred counterinsurgent formations. These communiqués from the rebellion offer clarity regarding the desperate and extraordinary victories, and the forms that the enemy will take. This text is a bearer of the summer's possibilities, proposals, and problems; I can imagine no better fate for writing. — **Joshua Clover**, author of *Riot.Strike.Riot: the New Era of Uprisings*.

The revolutionary meaning of the George Floyd uprising

Shemon Salam & Arturo Castillon

with a contribution from
Atticus Bagby-Williams

Daraja Press

2021

Published by Daraja Press
https://darajapress.com

Published in East Africa by Zand Graphics Ltd
https://zandgraphics.com/

Cover design: Kate McDonnell. Images: Shutterstock.com
ISBN 978-1-988832-95-1 (softcover) ISBN 9781988832968 (PDF)

Thinking Freedom: Series editor: Firoze Manji
Moving Beyond Capitalism - Now! Series editor: Howard Waitzkin
Cover design: Kate McDonnell;
Images: Shuttlestock.com (unless otherwise stated)

Thanks to *Ill Will Editions*, *Mute Magazine*, and *It's Going Down* for
publishing earlier versions of materials that we have updated and
revised here.

Library and Archives Canada Cataloguing in Publication
Title: The revolutionary meaning of the George Floyd uprisings / Shemon
    Salam & Arturo Castillon.
Names: Salam, Shemon, author. | Castillon, Arturo, 1988- author.
Description: Series statement: Thinking freedom
Identifiers: Canadiana (print) 20210113898 | Canadiana (ebook) 20210114088
    | ISBN 9781988832951 (softcover) | ISBN 9781988832968 (PDF)
Subjects: LCSH: Black lives matter movement. | LCSH: Protest movements
    —United States—History—21st
    century. | LCSH: Civil rights movements—United States—History—21st
    century. | LCSH: African
    Americans—Social conditions—21st century. | LCSH: United States—
    Race relations—History—21st
    century. | LCSH: Racism—United States—History—21st century. | LCSH:
    African Americans—Violence
    against. | LCSH: Racial profiling in law enforcement—United States. |
    LCSH: Police brutality—
    United States. | LCSH: Police shootings—United States.
Classification: LCC E185.615 .S25 2021 | DDC 323.1196/073—dc23

Contents

Preface

Arturo Castillon & Shemon Salam

LOS ANGELES – MAY 30, 2020: Police car attacked during the protest march against police violence over death of George Floyd.

At least 28 people died in the wave of social unrest that rocked the United States from late May until late July in 2020. In this 10-week period, there were 574 riots; 624 arsons; 2,382 incidents of looting; 97 police vehicles set on fire; and 16,241 people arrested for protest-related activities. In addition, at least 13 police were shot, 9 were hit by cars and 2,037 were reported injured in the riots, mostly because of the tossing of rocks, bricks, and other projectiles.[1]

In early May few would have predicted that by the end of that month widespread riots would sweep across the country. Even those expecting something like this were caught off guard by the sheer ferocity and intensity of the riots. Amid the Covid-19 pandemic, the lockdown, skyrocketing unemployment, and a rapidly deteriorating quality of life, the George Floyd uprising flashed across the sky like a blazing meteor, opening up a new chapter in the revolutionary history of the US proletariat[2] (or working class) which was finally joining the global wave of revolt that had convulsed the world—in places like Haiti, Sudan, Lebanon, and Chile—since 2019.

Beginning in Minneapolis on May 26th, the day after the video of the brutal police murder of George Floyd went viral, protesters began vandalizing the third precinct police station where the officer that murdered Floyd worked. The police dispersed the crowd using tear gas, but that night dozens of buildings were set on fire in the surrounding area. Over the next three days, the third precinct was overtaken and set ablaze, and hundreds of businesses were looted and burned throughout the Minneapolis and St. Paul metropolitan areas.[3] By May 30th, these tactics had generalized throughout much of the nation, with riots hitting almost every major city, as well as dozens of smaller cities and suburbs. Cop-cars, courthouses, municipal buildings, and retail stores all went up in flames.

The first two weeks of the uprising were unprecedented in terms of property destruction. By June 8th, a week and a half after the rebellion began in Minneapolis, people across the country had inflicted upwards of $2 billion in property damage—the highest recorded damage from social unrest in US history.[4] Though this included damage to some middle-class people's homes,

---

1. IMCCA Report, Intelligence Commander Group (October 2020) "Report on the 2020 Protests and Civil Unrest", Major Cities Chiefs Association (majorcitieschiefs.com).

2. By "proletariat" we mean all those who have nothing to lose but their chains, since they do not own capital in any form. Whether they make a lot of money, have a nice car, or pay a mortgage, if they are forced to sell their labor to a capitalist firm, the state, or small business in exchange for a wage, they are proletarians. Those who do unwaged work, those who are unemployed, and those involved in illegal economies are also proletarians.

3. Josh Sinner and MaryJo Webster (July 13, 2020) "Buildings Damaged in Minneapolis, St. Paul After Riots", Star Tribune.

4. Ariel Zilber (September 16, 2020) "George Floyd riots will cost insurance companies BILLION", Daily Mail (msn.com). Jennifer Kingson (September 16, 2020) "Exclusive: billion-plus riot damage is most expensive in insurance history", Axios.

most of the property damage was suffered by the capitalist class, big and small businesses alike, and to a lesser degree, the police state.

Police departments were quickly overwhelmed and out-maneuvered as multi-racial crowds stormed the commercial centers of countless cities, big and small. When police came to quell the rioting in one place, the crowd would break apart and spread the revolt elsewhere. In cities like Rockford, Chicago, Louisville, and Philadelphia, people formed looting caravans which travelled throughout the city and suburbs, converging on particular shopping centers and then driving off together to other locations.

By early June, 200 cities had imposed curfews.[5] Since it was clear that the police could not control the situation, at least 96,000 National Guard troops were mobilized in 34 states,[6] in addition to those that had already been deployed to the capital,[7] where protesters had clashed with Secret Service agents, injuring at least 50 of them, as others rushed President Trump into the bunker of the White House.[8] As the National Guard occupied dozens of cities throughout the country, the intensity and reach of the riots began to subside, while lawful, non-violent protests led by politicians and non-profit organizations began to dominate the political landscape once again. In contrast to the concrete actions of the uprising, these protests focused more on performative displays of radicalism, diversity, and anti-racist virtue, while shunning the illegal and confrontational tactics of the riots. Still, whether by carrot or stick, the counterinsurgency did not fully stamp out the insurrectionary upsurge of the proletariat. In response to continued instances of police violence, localized rebellions continued to pop up in specific cities, like Atlanta in mid-June; Portland throughout June and July; Chicago and Kenosha in August; Rochester, Lancaster, and Louisville in September; and Wauwatosa and Philadelphia in October.

The uprising in the streets merged with many other forms of struggle, including solidarity actions in workplaces and in prisons. For example in

---

5. Maria Sacchetti (June 1, 2020) "Curfews follow days of looting and demonstrations", *The Washington Post.*

6. National Guard Press Release (June 8, 2020) "National Guard response to civil unrest", the National Guard.

7. Victoria Bekiempis (July 3, 2020) "Troops sent to DC during George Floyd protests had bayonets, top general says", *The Guardian.* Julian Borger (June 1, 2020) "Fires light up Washington DC on third night of George Floyd protests", *The Guardian.*

8. Gregg Re (May 31, 2020) "Secret Service agents wounded outside White House, car bombs feared; official says Trump was taken to bunker", *Fox News.*

Chicago federal inmates banged on their windows and flashed their lights as protesters passed by.[9] In California, ICE detainees held a hunger strike in solidarity with the uprising.[10] The intersection between the uprising and workplace struggles was highlighted when bus driver unions in Minneapolis, San Francisco, New York, Philadelphia, and Washington DC refused to collaborate with the police in transporting detained protesters.[11] The uprising also coincided with a growing movement for housing, best exemplified in the occupation of a Sheraton hotel in Minneapolis in early June and its transformation into a homeless shelter.

As the riots and protests continued throughout the summer, workers continued to show support for the uprising. On June 19th, thousands of workers from the International Longshore and Warehouse Union as well as United Auto Workers stopped working for 8 minutes and 46 seconds, representing the amount of time that the cop that murdered George Floyd kneeled on his neck before he died. Then on July 20th, tens of thousands of workers in healthcare, transportation, food services, retail, education and other sectors walked off their jobs across the country.[12] There was also a wave of sports strikes in response to the rebellion that erupted in Kenosha in late August following the police shooting of Jacob Blake. In solidarity with the Kenosha rebellion, athletes refused to play in their scheduled sports events, from the National Basketball Association, to Major League Baseball, to Major League Soccer, to the Women's Tennis Association, to the National Hockey League.

The fact that the uprising reverberated far and wide reflects its depth and complexity. It was an autonomous movement, unmediated by any party, state, organization, or subculture. It was expansive, including anyone who was willing to take part in it. While the Black proletariat certainly led the charge, others also joined the fight, demonstrating new possibilities of multi-racial struggle. A new spirit of inter-racial solidarity was born in the streets as people came together to confront the authorities and watch them flee under a barrage

9.   Lauren Frias (May 29, 2020) "Watch inmates at a federal prison in downtown Chicago bang on walls and flash lights in solidarity with George Floyd protesters", *Insider*.

10. Fernie Ortiz (June 10, 2020) "ICE now says detainees held hunger strike in honor of George Floyd", *Border Report*.

11. Michelle Chen (June 5, 2020) "The Bus Drivers' Refusal", *Dissent Magazine*.

12. Rachel Treisman (July 20, 2020) "Essential Workers Hold Walkouts And Protests In National 'Strike For Black Lives" NPR.

of bottles, rocks, and bricks. It's an experience that is hard to forget. Despite the repression and counterinsurgency that ultimately prevailed, it's hard not to feel a new spirit of revolt, a certain mix of unity, defiance, and triumph. The uprising demonstrated that the existing order is not eternal or stable. There were thousands of young people in the streets willing to fight the police and take immense risks.

Beyond the moment of collective street action, however, the movement began to run into clear limits that couldn't be ignored. Aside from the predictable white racist backlash and mounting state violence, one of the greatest challenges that prevented the deepening of the uprising was the rise of a Black led counterinsurgency. The Black leaders who took a hard stand against the illegal and violent aspects of the uprising were very effective in co-opting the revolutionary fervor of masses of proletarians and forcing the politics of the movement back into the bounds of reformism. Furthermore, there were also clear limits to the uprising when it came to gender. When it was time to riot for Breonna Taylor, few were willing to fight as hard as they had for George Floyd. We consider these and other uncomfortable truths in the opening text, "Race, Class, and Gender in the 2020 Uprising." While grappling with these contradictions, we also focus on what we see as the insurgent self-activity of the class. This is the starting point for any attempt to overcome the internal limits of the movement, which ultimately can only be worked out in the process of mass struggle.

With this background about the strengths and contradictions of the uprising, we turn to several other key developments. The second text, "Cars, Riots, and Black Liberation" provides a first-hand reflection on the Walter Wallace rebellion in Philadelphia, where the Black proletariat refined the tactic of looting by car, one of the greatest tactical innovations of the uprising. The third text, "Prelude to a New Civil War", traces the mounting hostilities of the uprising back to the unfinished business of the first US Civil War. A controversial position for some, we argue that the tensions and contours of the 2020 riots indicate the unique relationship between civil war and revolution that is so pronounced in the United States. The fourth text, "Fire on Main Street", looks at how the uprising played out in small cities and suburbs throughout the country, focusing on the strategic implications that these peripheral areas pose for questions of insurrection and revolution. The final text in the collection, "Postscript on the 2020 Riots", looks at some of the developments that defined the end of the uprising, namely the rise of right-wing, pro-Trump riots in the context of Joe Biden's presidential election.

1

Class, Race and Gender in the 2020 Uprising

ARTURO CASTILLON AND SHEMON SALAM

While it is clear enough that the George Floyd uprising was a response to racism, specifically anti-Black racism, it must be emphasized that this was also a class conflict the likes of which our generation has never seen. While the anti-police riots were generally initiated by proletarian Black people, it's also true that white, Latinx, Asian, and Indigenous people all fought in the uprising. It wasn't just a Black uprising but also an uprising of young white people and other racialized groups. This dialectic between Black liberation and universal revolt is what gave the uprising its immense potential—unemployed, precarious wage-laborers, blue-collar workers, and middle-class renegades all coalesced in a multi-racial battle against the state and bourgeois society.

At the same time, we can't ignore the uncomfortable fact that much of the counterinsurgency was led by Black police, Black politicians, Black owned businesses, and Black non-profits, which played a key role in co-opting the uprising. When these groups showed up to the protests and scorned the illegal tactics of the proletariat, militants who were ready to riot often went home, unsure of whether they would receive any political support from these officials of the movement. Alongside the raw violence of the police and paramilitaries, the reactionary politics of the Black led counterinsurgency helped force the horizon of the uprising back into the bounds of budget reforms and electoral politics. As the summer wore on and the counterinsurgency went into full swing, the riots became less frequent, and racial boundaries were increasingly reimposed by a loose alliance of "white allies" and "Black leaders" working in tandem with local politicians, non-profits, and businesses.

Alongside race and class, gender also defined the internal dynamics of the uprising, as women, men, and people of all genders took part in the riots. But if it was anti-Black racism and the class oppression of Black proletarians that initially set off the uprising, it was through the contradiction of gender that it began to come to a close. In the case of the Breonna Taylor protests that followed on the heels of the initial George Floyd uprising, it seemed like fewer proletarians were willing to come out and fight for Breonna. The George Floyd uprising was shot through with these and other contradictions. Without accounting for them, we cannot hope to fully understand the internal dynamics of the uprising, much less develop its insurgent possibilities.

A Multi-Racial Uprising Led by the Black Proletariat

Frequent cases of racist police violence in the US, especially against Black Americans, have long resulted in rebellions like those that took place throughout the 1960s, the 1992 Los Angeles riots, Ferguson in 2014, Baltimore in 2015, Baton Rouge and St. Paul in 2016. What's unique about the 2020 riots, however, is the degree to which non-Black people participated. Most surprising was the large number of whites who took part. Of course, this wasn't the first time that white people rebelled alongside Black people, but still, white participation in the 2020 riots was far more pronounced than previous cycles of riots, demonstrating that whiteness could no longer be counted on to hold all the whites together as a counter-revolutionary bloc. The 2020 riots revealed a layer of white people who we can describe as "race-traitors"—radical white anti-racists who fought (and even died) alongside militants of color in the uprising.[1]

The George Floyd uprising was layered by many interrelated crises, including police brutality, mass incarceration, and anti-Black racism, but also

---

1. For more on the theory of white race-traitors see our text, "The Return of John Brown: White Race-Traitors in the 2020 Uprising", published on September 4th, 2020 by *Ill Will Editions* (illwilleditions.com).

the Covid-19 pandemic, and the more general crisis of capitalism. It's in the context of these intertwined crises that we must situate the expansive multi-racial dynamics of the uprising. The class divide between the proletariat and bourgeoisie has deepened considerably since the 1970s and the current proletariat has suffered decades of deindustrialization, declining wages, deepening poverty, financial crises, and jobless recoveries. On top of all these downward trends, the Covid-19 pandemic has drastically lowered the proletariat's living standards and created the worst global recession since the 1930s. When you add the uneven racial impact that all these structural crises have on Black and Latinx people, the result is a large and highly diverse cross-section of very dissatisfied and very unruly proletarians.

A Black-Led Counterinsurgency

As the summer went on, the Black counterinsurgency was a decisive force in halting the momentum of the uprising. In the absence of a larger milieu of Black revolutionaries, few militants were willing to defy the Black liberals who, far from siding with the Black proletariat in revolt, were openly hostile to it. This was not a local phenomenon in one or two cities, but a dynamic that played out across the nation. When Black politicians, Black police leaders, and Black nonprofits showed up and began denouncing the illegal aspects of the uprising, many obeyed and fell in line. Even though the Black proletariat continued to launch sporadic rebellions throughout the summer and fall, some opponents of the uprising went so far as to claim that outside agitators were responsible for all the unrest, a narrative well within mainstream consensus. When wielded by respectable Black leaders, this narrative was especially effective in discouraging further revolt.

The problems that led to the fires of 2020 would certainly have been easy to resolve if outsiders or provocateurs were responsible, but this narrative only obscured the reality that this was a multi-racial uprising against a multi-racial ruling class. It was an uprising of Black proletarians and their multi-racial allies against a multi-racial, largely Democratic, urban establishment that often included Black politicians, Black police, Black capitalists, and Black non-profits. This was the case in Minneapolis, Chicago, Kenosha, Philadelphia, Atlanta, Birmingham, Tampa and many other cities. No doubt, behind the Black elite lies billion-dollar philanthropies, universities, the state, and ultimately, the white elite. Still, this doesn't change the fact that a Black-led counterinsurgency played a leading role in neutralizing an uprising led by the Black proletariat.

This argument might be shocking to some, but it reflects concrete material changes that have come about since the 1960s, in particular the hardening of class tensions among Black people. Of course, this isn't entirely new—the uprisings of the 1960s had already revealed a growing conflict between the Black proletariat and a small Black elite. Over the decades, this class conflict has only deepened, reaching new heights in the 2020 riots.

Gender in the Uprising

The police murdered Breonna Taylor in March 2020 as they served a no-knock warrant at her house in Louisville, Kentucky. The protests and actions that took place following the announcement of the verdict in that case were arguably the least militant of any of the major protests in 2020. Why? Why did people not fight as hard for Breonna as they had for George? Was it because the momentum of the uprising was over by the time the protests happened in late September? Was it because the National Guard prevented a rebellion? Or was it simply because the movement won't fight as hard when the police murder a Black woman?

The most obvious explanation is that there was no viral video of the incident that led to Breonna Taylor's death. In contrast, there was a very brutal and detailed video of George Floyd's murder. While this factor might have much to do with why people feel more compelled to riot in one case and not another, we can also point out that plenty of anti-police rebellions have happened when there was no video, especially before the 1992 Los Angeles riots. There was no video when people in Chicago rioted and looted in response to the police shooting of Latrell Allen in early August 2020.

Then there's the argument that the momentum of the uprising was starting to wane by the time they announced the verdict in late September. This is certainly a factor. The initial uprising was on a downward trend at this point. Yet localized rebellions were still happening—there were two very intense rebellions in Wauwatosa and Philadelphia the next month, in October. So, the argument that the momentum of the riots was over, also doesn't hold up.

The fact that the National Guard occupied Louisville in anticipation of the protests is a big factor behind the lack of militancy. As would happen with Kenosha in early January of 2021 following the verdict on the cop who shot Jacob Blake, the National Guard was able to prevent a rebellion in Louisville by preemptively occupying the city. Both Louisville and Kenosha confirmed that when the state anticipates a riot and is actively prepared for it, it is almost impossible for the proletariat to defeat the state. Unable to riot in downtown Louisville, Black proletarians began looting in a few areas on the outskirts of the city, but that was it.

Similar to Minneapolis, Kenosha, Portland, or Seattle, Louisville is a majority white city. Unlike the George Floyd riots that happened in these places in Louisville in late May, however, white proletarians were noticeably absent during the Breonna Taylor protests in late September. This signaled a shift in the composition of the riots, from multi-racial to Black, a divergence which would repeat itself in the rebellions in Wauwatosa and Philadelphia in October. If the multi-racial proletariat went on the offensive in the summer and sporadically in the beginning of the fall, by the middle of the fall it seemed like only the most insurgent elements of the Black proletariat were still willing to riot. It seems like the crucial shift happened in September. While there was a multi-racial rebellion in Lancaster, Pennsylvania, in the beginning of September, this trend seemed to stop by the end of that month.

So, what does the lack of a rebellion in Louisville tell us about gender in the uprising?

It's inescapable that the most militant anti-police revolts so far have been about the murder of Black men. While we can interpret this as a sign of patriarchy, it also reflects the basic fact that, aside from Indigenous men, Black men are the most likely people to be incarcerated and murdered by the police. If we want to break it down by gender, 1,377 Black men have been murdered by police since 2015, in contrast to 48 Black women.[2] Given the disproportionate level of police violence that Black men experience, it shouldn't come as a surprise that this group is the driving force behind most anti-police rebellions.

---

2.   "Police shootings database 2015-2021", *The Washington Post*.

In an attempt to stop people from rioting, activist peace-police[3] accuse men rioters of endangering women and children, affirming non-violence in their name. This line of thinking reduces women to passive bystanders to men's rage and violence, when in fact women were active participants in the uprising. While the common logic is that men are the fighters and women are the care-takers, the uprising exploded this binary, showing us that women weren't only providing medical aid and food and other forms of social reproduction, but were also smashing windows, fighting cops, starting fires, and looting. A cursory look at those arrested in the riots last year confirms this.[4] Now, we are certainly not denying the monopoly of violence that men wield in a patriarchal society. While we are hesitant to reach generalizations, our experience is that Black men took a leading role in the looting, property destruction, and street fighting during the uprising. We can acknowledge this, and the reasons for it, while at the same time recognizing the Black women in Philadelphia and Chicago who were looting and fighting the cops, or the Black women in Louisville who were openly carrying pistols and rifles during the Breonna Taylor protests. While many believe that rioting and looting are inherently masculine, anarchist militant Vicky Osterweil has pointed out how these activities can actually be quite feminine.[5]

To summarize: elements of the Black proletariat responded with some armed marches and a few nights of looting in Louisville, but the Breonna Taylor protests did not develop into a full-blown rebellion. This was the result of a combination of various factors which came together to limit the insurgent potential of the protests:

1. *Preemptive repression.* The National Guard preemptively occupied Louisville, making the proletariat lose the element of surprise (as it also did in Kenosha in early January 2021).

2. *The narrowing composition of the riots.* The composition of the riots changed significantly from the beginning of September, when a multi-racial riot erupted in Lancaster, Pennsylvania. In contrast, by the end of September, only the most militant sections of the Black

---

3. "Peace-police" are protesters who try to stop other protesters from engaging in illegal tactics like looting, property destruction, fighting the police, etc.

4. Michael Loadenthal (July 1, 2020) "Tracking federal cases related to Summer protests, riots, & uprisings", *The Prosecution Project.*

5. Zoe Samudzi (June 10, 2020) "Stealing Away in America", *Jewish Currents.*

proletariat were still in revolt.

3. *The marginalization of Black women in the struggle against the police.* The proletariat generally does not riot when Black women are murdered by police. While on the one hand this reflects a major limit in regard to gender, including the failure to recognize and amplify women militants, on the other hand, this also reflects the basic fact that Black men are disproportionately murdered by police.

Conclusion

Over and over again during the 2020 uprising, proletarians of all colors and genders joined together to smash the police state and loot capitalism. It took the National Guard occupying dozens of cities throughout the country to bring the initial uprising to an end, and even then, localized rebellions continued to emerge throughout the fall. The radical alliances that emerged in the streets upended common sense notions of gender, class, race, solidarity, politics, and organization. However, this movement also ran into clear limits as the counterinsurgency went into effect and the shared unity in the streets dissipated.

If we are going to prepare for the next upsurge of resistance, we will have to engage with the internal contradictions sketched out in this text, among them the rise of a Black-led counterinsurgency, declining white participation in the riots, as well as the tendency to frame the riots as male-centric while ignoring the women who took part. Still, whether we are able to overcome these internal limits largely depends on whether proletarians are willing to address them in the process of struggling together against their common class enemies. Revolutionaries can help make this happen by articulating a strategy of revolutionary struggle that directly tackles the specific contradictions of gender, race and class within the movement.

2

Cars, Riots, and Black Liberation

Lessons from Philadelphia's Walter Wallace Rebellion

SHEMON SALAM AND ARTURO CASTILLON

> *"The working class in every country lives its own life, makes its own experiences,*
> *seeking always to create forms and realize values which originate*
> *directly from its organic opposition to official society."*
> —CLR James, Grace Lee Boggs, and Cornelius Castoriadis, *Facing Reality*[1]

Glass shatters. Thick plumes of dark black smoke pour out of a burning police car stalled in the middle of 52nd street. Another Black man shot dead by the police. Another rebellion in defense of basic human dignity. "Sir, it's chaos!" one of the officers yells into his radio as they retreat under a barrage of rocks, bottles, bricks. "Stop throwing shit!" an older black man yells, but the young black militants keep throwing projectiles anyway. The police, outnumbered by the hundreds, can only watch from a distance as large groups of people loot the stores all along the Ave. The cops concentrate on blocking off major intersections.

While stuck in a traffic jam, waiting for the red light to turn green, a car breaks whatever is left of the law and speeds away. Time and speed do not obey red, yellow, or green here. This is no ordinary traffic jam. It is the traffic jam of Black liberation, where

---

1.   CLR James, Grace Lee Boggs, and Cornelius Castoriadis: *Facing Reality*. Detroit: Bewick Editions, 1974

looting by car is the art form developed in response to the murder of Walter Wallace Jr. by the Philadelphia Police.

All of a sudden, a group of teenagers pop out of a car and walk down the street to an unknown destination. Cop-cars zoom past them in a panic of sirens, red and blue lights flashing through the night, probably rushing to another 911 call about looters at a pharmacy, Footlocker, grocery store, or liquor store somewhere else. Across the street, a gas station is filled with cars of young Black people hopping in and out, discussions taking place, and music blaring. It is part music festival, part pit-stop, and part modern day proletarian council where young people discuss what to do next.

What happened in Ferguson in 2014 as an impromptu practice has now become an art in Philadelphia: the art of looting by car. The official record will simply list this activity as crime that has nothing to do with politics. But there could be nothing further from the truth. Black rioters are the creators of new tactics of struggle, new visions of liberation, and new types of revolutionary organization. The accomplishments of the rebellion in Philadelphia were powerful, liberating, and simply beautiful. While pundits will dismiss the riots as apolitical or criminal, it is the radical activities of the Black proletariat that create the very political conditions that put revolutionary change on the horizon.

Protesters use forklift to loot washing machine in West Philadelphia during the George Floyd uprising, June 1st, 2020 (private photo)

Ignoring the Strategic Implications of the Uprising

In order to oppose it and crush it, the state and far-right are forced to take the uprising very seriously. But for the liberals and moderates that wish to make the uprising respectable in the eyes of bourgeois society, 93 percent of the George Floyd protests have been baptized as peaceful and lawful.[2] Using this statistical sleight of hand, liberalism and reformism equates the Black Lives Matter movement with non-violent, legal protest, while writing off the illegal and violent actions of the masses of proletarians who took part in the uprising. Even socialists have stuck their heads in the sand when it comes to the tactical and strategic implications of the riots. Meanwhile Black proletarians are taking immense risks in a battle of life and death.

Everyone condemns racism and police brutality in the abstract, but for all their claims of solidarity with Black liberation, most leftists fall miserably short when it comes to directly supporting and participating in the revolutionary activities of the Black proletariat. If we are serious about revolution, then there are no excuses. Whether it's distributing food to insurgents, providing medical support, gathering and distributing riot materials, listening to the police scanner and relaying information, providing transportation, safehouses, and legal support, or just doing the actual rioting, looting, and street fighting, everyone has a role to play. At this point in the development of class tensions and the deepening crisis of capitalism, we can expect to see more rebellions in the near future. The question is, are we willing to prepare ourselves accordingly?

If the uprising taught us anything, it's that solidarity with the movement means risking your skin. This is easy to forget when the law has expanded in response to class conflicts and anti-racist struggles to the point that plenty of harmless forms of activism can be engaged in. We can safely denounce racism, police brutality, and war, march almost anywhere we wish, and say whatever we want to the authorities. This range of legality might seem like a victory, but it has also become a trap that leftist organizations treat as a principle. The reality is that leftist organizations are simply not prepared to deal with the illegal nature of the struggles that are taking place in the present moment. Leftists run their mouths about organizational questions in abstract and antiquated terms, regurgitating a played-out formula modeled on Russia or China that has been repeated ad nauseam, but which has produced little more than sects and cults. They ignore the concrete revolutionary activities that are already taking place. Organizational, tactical, and strategic clarity is

---

2.   Major Cities Chiefs Association, Intelligence Commander Group (October 2020) "Report on the 2020 Protests and Civil Unrest", www.majorcitieschiefs.com

emerging for the first time since the 1960s, but it is not coming from the left—it is coming from the practical initiatives of the Black proletariat, which continues to show a practical commitment to fighting the police and looting the commodities of this dying capitalist system. When these are the tactics of the proletariat in its battle with class society, what kind of organizational forms make sense?

Revolutionary organizations are not built in the abstract but are expressions of the tactical and strategic challenges raised by the proletariat in the process of class struggle. The fundamental organizational question that revolutionaries now face is how to contribute and relate to the coming riots and uprisings. In order to do so, those who are truly committed to revolution will have to move beyond the stale organizational forms of the past and begin to account for the diverse, illegal, and creative forms that the Black proletariat has developed, the use of cars being one of the most innovative tools in this emerging tactical practice.

The official understanding of this moment is that the rioters are unorganized, lack direction, and need leadership. The reality that many activists continually fail to recognize is that forms of coordination and organization are already happening within the maelstrom of the riot. This should be obvious when large caravans of looters swarm specific locations at the same time. It cannot be completely spontaneous that Black proletarians converged on Wal-Mart, looted it, and when the cops arrived, evaded them and went on to form convoys of up to thirty cars that targeted multiple shopping districts throughout the city. The question of revolutionary organization, then, is not a matter of bringing organization to those who have none, but of connecting and engaging with the organic forms of organization that emerge through the autonomous actions of the proletariat.

New Dynamics, New Divisions

Revolutionary organizations prove themselves in the battle of class conflict. In the case of Philadelphia, any revolutionary organization had to deal with the dynamics of feet and tires. Of course, most people rioted and looted on foot. But as the 2020 riots wore on, and the state became more prepared for prolonged street confrontations, it became harder to continue on foot. In response, some rioters used cars to outmaneuver the police and spread the rebellion to other areas. We had already seen this in early August following the murder of Latrell Allen in Chicago, where rioters formed car caravans that looted the Magnificent Mile. This trend continued in Louisville with the Breonna Taylor protests in late September, where state preparation made an uprising in the city practically impossible. In response, people took to cars and spread the riots geographically by looting businesses on the periphery of the city. These were brilliant tactical innovations when facing the raw power of the state.

Car looting has clear advantages to looting on foot. There's less peace policing because there is not as much of an association with a specific geography, and what is often the same thing, a specific race. The most important aspect of car-looting, however, is that it disperses and exhausts the police. This strategy can create a dynamic where those left on foot find themselves in de facto police free zones, able to revel in freedom for extended periods of time, because the police are too busy trying to counter the looting caravans elsewhere. This is what happened in Philadelphia. The synergy of those on foot and those in cars created a different geography and dynamic of struggle where police cars were racing from store to store trying to stop the roving bands of car-looters, while those on foot found themselves pulling police resources in a different direction. There were simply too many rioters in different places and not enough police.

We also can't ignore the use of cars as riot weapons. While we've seen cops and right-wingers use cars against BLM protesters, there were also several incidents during the uprising in which cars were used as weapons against the police. This happened in Philadelphia, among other cities. Police were hit and run over during the Walter Wallace Rebellion, as also occurred during the George Floyd riots in Philadelphia over the summer.

The use of cars in riots generates several strategic advantages, but the car is certainly not a perfect tool. The license plate is a huge security risk. With a few keystrokes police can use your license plate to look up your address and knock on your door. While this presents many dangers, what's important to note is that proletarians are finding ways to loot by car and not get caught regardless. Besides the risks that come with having a license plate, evading the police by car is oftentimes more dangerous than on foot, and getting caught after a high-speed chase is going to result in longer jail time.

Aside from the security risks, the second problem is that you need a car in the first place, or at least need to know someone who has a car. While car ownership is widespread in the US, it is largely determined by race and class. According to a study from the University of California, "African Americans have the lowest car ownership of all racial and ethnic groups in the country", the researchers say, "with 19 percent living in homes in which no one owns a car. That compares to 4.6 percent of whites in homes with no car, 13.7 percent of Latinos, and 9.6 percent of the remaining groups combined." While not having your own car is probably not a total barrier, taking note of the unequal ownership of cars is important. At the same time, the fact that car-looting has so far been almost entirely Black shows us the determination of Black proletarians to use cars in the uprising.

The third concern is that the car can atomize the struggle, where each car is a separate unit. While in a way, this dynamic socializes the specific rioters within each car, it does so in a very different manner than looting on foot, where there is much more of a social and collective atmosphere. In contrast to looting on foot as part of a large crowd, each car functions as a ship unto itself, making it difficult to engage with drivers and passengers in other cars. Furthermore, if you aren't already part of the caravan of looters, joining a random car caravan can invite suspicion, especially if the caravan is made up of friends who already know each other. But if you can figure out how to participate, these limits can be broken down in the rush of doors opening, looters jumping in and out of cars.

If the initial division of the uprising was between legal and illegal protests, non-violent and violent protests, good and bad protesters, it is clear that another division has emerged: shoes versus tires. However, unlike the division between lawful and criminal protesters, this division is not an obstacle to the deepening of the struggle. Unlike previous divisions which reflected class, race, and political differences in the movement, this one emerges directly out of the tactical back and forth between the police and the Black proletariat. This organic division arises in response to the maneuvers of the police, and therefore, reflects innovation and creativity, instead of containment and counterinsurgency.

New Geographies of Struggle

If the initial phase of the uprising this summer was concentrated on the wealthiest portions of cities, in the fall the proletariat abandoned Jefferson Square Park in Louisville, and abandoned Center City in Philly, and instead used cars to spread the rebellion geographically. Instead of fixating on a specific territory, those who looted by car used the vastness of urban space to create new territories of struggle. This reflects a qualitative change in the class struggle that still needs to be accounted for.

A century ago, it was factories which dotted the terrain of class struggle. Today it is the shopping district, the cell phone store, the CVS, and the Apple store that mark the new geography of struggle. Riots and looting, therefore, are not the result of delusions on the part of the proletariat but are instead reflections of what capital looks like now: wealth in the form of commodities concentrated in key neighborhoods, often spread geographically throughout cities. While these commodities are not the means of production, they certainly represent a vast collection of wealth just waiting to be expropriated. The looting of Wal-Mart is an excellent example of this. Here capital has brought together a vast assemblage of commodities which proletarians usually have to pay for. The mass looting of Wal-Mart in Port Richmond (Northeast Philadelphia) on October 27th and 28th was precisely the reaction of people who are forced to live and work alongside this hyper-concentration of commodities. Instead of dismissing riots as unorganized or "unstrategic", then, it makes more sense to ask why proletarians in the United States are rioting more than they're striking.

Precise data are not available of what kind of jobs rioters hold, but an educated guess is that if they hold jobs, they are most likely in low-wage service sector jobs with little structural power. Unlike factory strikes, strikes in restaurants or retail stores might shut down those particular businesses, but this has little impact on the overall economy. While it is safe to assume that these proletarians are taking their radical experiences in the uprising back into their workplaces, these workplaces are not the giant factories which incubated the revolutionary forces of the past. Instead of identifying as workers and deriving their power from their workplaces, these proletarians find street riots, even those that result in the destruction of their workplaces, to be more powerful than struggles within the workplace. This is not by accident or because of "false consciousness" but is instead an expression of the changing nature of work and the current composition of the proletariat. It is also an expression of where proletarians feel their power lies.

The Car as a Weapon of Black Liberation

While many on the left correctly criticize cars as climate-destroying machines, there is an alternative history of the car that we must pay attention to. The Montgomery Bus Boycott in 1955-56 is perhaps the most famous example. Civil rights activists, particularly Black women who were domestic workers, organized an alternative public transportation system based on cars in order to boycott the segregation of the buses in Montgomery, Alabama. This history provides valuable lessons for our current moment, especially when it comes to the question of social reproduction.

If we begin with the 2014 Ferguson uprising,[3] we see cars being used as getaway vehicles, as barriers to create police free zones, and as shields to fire at cops. But cars in Ferguson were not used for the purposes of spreading the uprising geographically. Instead, spaces were defended around several sites in Ferguson, most importantly the QT and Canfield and West Florissant. Compared to the 2010s, the riots happening today have escalated in intensity and expanded in geography, the looting convoy being the best example of this.

Dozens of gas guzzling monsters roaring down the streets, tires screeching, tinted windows, speeding through red lights—this is the caravan of Black liberation.

A crucial aspect of the moving wave of mass struggles, the looting caravan can be understood through the framework of Rosa Luxemburg's great text, *the Mass Strike*. While many communists agree with Luxemburg today, it was a controversial argument that she was making at the time. Luxemburg challenged the widely held conception of how socialism would come about in the 2nd International: a peaceful evolution won by the vote. Instead, she demonstrated that the strike waves rolling through Eastern Europe were the key to socialism. While it would be foolish to claim that looting convoys alone will get us to a classless society, this form of struggle is nonetheless one of the most innovative responses to a variety of tactical, strategic, and political economic developments of our time. How this form of struggle will connect to

---

3.   Avalanche (November 2014) "Guns, Cars, and Autonomy", *The Anarchist Library.*

communism is not fully clear, but it is communistic in the sense of its mass nature and its uncompromising attack on the commodity form.

What we see from Ferguson to Philadelphia is the growing use of the car as a weapon of mass struggle. In Ferguson in 2014, cars were used for defensive purposes, while in Chicago, Louisville, Philadelphia, and elsewhere in 2020, cars were used for offensive purposes: for looting, for attacking police, and for spreading the geography of the uprising. We should expect cars to continue to play an important role as riots continue to unfold and potentially mutate into other forms of mass struggle: blockades, strikes, and occupations. Undoubtedly, the state will respond with new forms of surveillance and repression, but how it will do that is still unclear. In the meantime, Black proletarians will probably take advantage of the state's lack of capacity to deal with widespread looting by car. As revolutionaries, it is our duty to participate in this emerging form of struggle, to defend it, to help it grow and spread, and to articulate its potentials and limits.

3

Prelude to a New Civil War

SHEMON SALAM AND ARTURO CASTILLON

It was the proletarian general strike of the ex-slaves that truly put the final nail in the coffin of slavery.
It is precisely this lineage of an emancipatory, liberatory, but nonetheless violent, civil war that needs to be updated for its second coming.
—Idris Robinson, "How It Might Should Be Done"[1]

As indicated in poll after poll, op-ed after op-ed, more and more Americans are thinking about the present in terms of civil war. Why? The legacy of the US Civil War is an obvious reason, but why is the specter of civil war raised so vigorously today? Why do so many people see the escalation of partisan conflict as inevitable?

This sentiment cannot be separated from the fires of the George Floyd uprising, which itself has unfolded in the context of decades of deindustrialization, the rise of mass incarceration, the 2008 economic crisis, the Trump presidency, and now, the ravages of the Covid-19 pandemic, which triggered a deepening of poverty and unemployment, but also anti-police riots across the country. The conjunction of all these events reveals deep splits within American society which any strategy for revolution will have to account for.

---

1.   Idris Robinson (July 20, 2020) "How It Might Should Be Done", Ill Will Editions.

Since the end of May we've seen that Black proletarians won't hesitate to riot in response to the murderous actions of the police. The anti-police riot coalesces into a multi-racial insurgency, which, in turn, provokes repression and counterinsurgency, and not just from the police, but also from right-wing paramilitaries, and even from moderates and liberals. The deepening of this social conflict—between those who support the uprising and those who oppose it—raises the question of civil war in a concrete manner; it fractures the unified bloc of whiteness, but also the racial politics of other groups as well, including Black people, as shown in the division between Black partisans of revolt and Black counterinsurgents. In the fight for life and dignity, the Black proletariat in motion splits society in a particular way, resulting in a form of civil war which is not just a matter of rhetoric or metaphor, but a real material contradiction that encapsulates the American form of class war and which is inseparable from race.

For now, civil war remains latent; it has not yet become a historical event. Still, the signs of mass polarization are visible everywhere: the politics of fear, paranoia, contempt, and hate are manifest in the everyday behaviors and opinions of large swaths of US society. It is less the fact of civil war than the threat of its potential that attracts and repels, expands and limits, inspires and frightens the collective imagination. Few say it in public, but in the privacy of their homes, people again ask themselves: are we on the eve of a civil war?

Interpretations

As the far-right sees it, they are building the forces that can intervene and put an end to the threat posed by the uprising. These forces are even willing to break the law and engage in their own forms of insurgent tactics in order to uphold their vision of unbridled US capitalism. In fact, a substantial portion of right-wingers believe that the George Floyd uprising was the opening salvo in a new sequence of civil war. Militant formations like the Michigan Home Guard, the 3 Percenters, the Proud Boys, and the Boogaloo Boys are some of the most violent and radical forces on the right to take up the fight.

By contrast, the left generally avoids the question of civil war all together. Except for a tiny minority (e.g., Robert Evans' "It Could Happen Here",[2] Kali

---

2. https://podcasts.apple.com/ca/podcast/it-could-happen-here/id1449762156

Akuno,[3] and the Revolutionary Abolitionist Movement[4]), most on the left do not conceive of the present moment in terms of civil war, because the potential dangers are too much to bear. Since the overwhelming majority of guns are in the hands of right-wingers, and they generally garner more sympathy from the state, many leftists worry that a civil war will lead to a massacre of the most oppressed. While one part of the left believes that the Biden presidency can prevent a civil war, another part is hoping that the riots will open up the possibility of revolution and that they can skip over a civil war entirely. Meanwhile, the far right continues to radicalize, becoming more militant, and continues to gun down BLM protestors and run them over with cars. It is no surprise that a minority of leftists have had enough and are also coming to protests armed.

There is no imaginable scenario in which an electoral or policy fix succeeds in resolving the long crisis of US capitalism, the devastation wrought by the pandemic, the persistence of racist police violence, and the heightening of political tensions. Proletarians are going to continue to riot against inequality and police violence, while the far-right is going to continue to become inflamed.

The Structure of Revolution in the USA

If the specter of civil war haunts the American political landscape, this is because the Civil War era was by far the most revolutionary event in American history. However, because revolution and civil war are often framed in opposition to each other, we forget that a revolution did indeed take place. Black former slaves and poor whites in the South temporarily united during the Civil War to carry out a revolution that overthrew slavery. As newly freed people struggled with former plantation owners, whites and Blacks even created something akin to a commune in the Free State of Jones in Mississippi, while freed people took control of their destiny on the Sea Islands. At the same time, this revolutionary current triggered a counter-revolution that played out

---

3.   See, for example, https://cooperationjackson.org/announcementsblog/2017/1/8/heres-how-we-prepare-to-be-ungovernable-in-2017

4.   See, for example, https://truthout.org/articles/burning-down-the-american-plantation-an-interview-with-the-revolutionary-abolitionist-movement/

over the course of the Reconstruction era, ultimately leading to the defeat of any semblance of interracial democracy.

While it is not remembered in this way, the US Civil War was just as revolutionary as the 1871 Paris Commune, the 1917 Russian Revolution, or the 1949 Chinese Revolution. Rather than anarchism, socialism, or national liberation, however, the synthesis of race and class in the United States revealed a unique form of revolution marked by the three-fold dynamic of civil war, abolition, and reconstruction. This emancipatory tradition is itself rooted in centuries of slave revolts, marronage, and everyday resistance to slavery.

We are a country that has never had an anarchist or communist revolution, but we have had a revolution in the form of a civil war against racialized capitalist slavery. Why was there never a communist or anarchist revolution in the USA? In our view, the answer to that question lies in the particular history of whiteness and the failure of working class struggles to overcome it. As WEB Dubois first argued in *Black Reconstruction,* the possibilities of multi-racial struggle were marred by "the wages of whiteness." Even though their class realities sharply diverged, white workers struck a devil's bargain with the white elite: in exchange for preferential treatment based on race, white workers would agree to police and discipline the Black proletariat and other proletarians of color. This amounted to a cross-class alliance between the capitalist elite and the white proletariat, against the rest of the proletariat. Although there were challenges to this racial structure, it nonetheless became the glue that held class society together in the US. As the movement and formation of the US proletariat became divided along the color line, the structure of class conflict in the US became centered around race.

While legal slavery was abolished, racial capitalism took new forms. The defeat of chattel slavery heralded a century of Jim Crow legislation, while the fundamental social questions that the Civil War had raised—land, housing, education, healthcare— continued to be denied to masses of Black people. As the 1960s Civil Rights movement managed to remove many legal barriers, this allowed the rise of a Black middle-class compatible with the needs of capitalism and the state, while Black proletarians were left to fend for themselves.

To this day, the revolutionary tasks of the US Civil War remain unfinished, and the fact that its specter has arisen again is no coincidence: race continues to mediate class, not only in people's experiences, but also in the specific organization of class society. This tension is inherent to the United States. But while much of the radical left recognizes that race is inseparable from capitalism, as soon as this is applied to class struggle and revolution, race fades away and dogma comes to the front. If we really see race as central, this should change the forms that both class and revolution take. In the spirit of Fanon, we have to "stretch" our analysis of class in order to make sense of the dynamics of race. When we do so, we will see that race fundamentally shapes the contours of class conflict and revolution.

Then and Now

The structure of revolution in the USA is determined by the dynamics of the First Civil War, yet it is a mistake to superimpose the past on the present. The United States is very different than it was in the 19th century. The first civil war had a rising bourgeoisie in the Republican Party and the North. They were riding the expansion of capitalism, carrying them well into the 20th century. There is no foreseeable dynamic paralleling that process today. The US bourgeoisie and capitalism are in severe crisis. The pandemic has triggered a new recession and a deepening of the downward economic trends that began during the 2008 crisis. There was no V shaped recovery then and there will be none now. Furthermore, the Democratic Party is continuing its course of neoliberalism, and Biden has denied every plank of the popular social movements: universal healthcare, the Green New Deal, and #Defund.

During and after the first US Civil War, the federal government provided the troops and material resources that defended Black people during Reconstruction. This certainly closed many radical horizons, but at the same time, it was the only strategy free Black people could pursue. As long as masses of poor whites were not willing to fight alongside free Black people, the federal government was the devil Black people had to make alliances with. The legacy of Reconstruction has left behind a powerful "Black" social democratic tradition rooted in mass movements, one that ultimately needs to be overcome if we want a revolution. The only way masses of Black people can overcome this tradition is by seeing a new horizon open up through multi-racial insurrectionary struggle. This can simultaneously solve the race, the state, and the political economic question.

The first civil war was a contest between two distinct regions of the United States which both had industrial and food producing capacities. A modern-day civil war would have a radically different geography. It would not be North versus South. It would be a conflict within each metropolis, each city, each town, each suburb, in each state and region. Of course, an intense polarization is to be expected in places like Portland and Seattle, where political conflict has been particularly pronounced of late. But conflicts will also emerge in smaller cities, towns, and suburbs with very little recent history of rebellion, as we already saw during the George Floyd uprising. Smaller cities like Kenosha, Rochester, and Lancaster have a larger concentration of racist whites and smaller sized police departments, making them some of the most volatile sites of potential civil war. Whereas in big cities people of color are a larger section of society, and racist whites tend to hide behind the police, in the small cities and suburbs people of color can find themselves surrounded by a sea of whites who are often ready to engage in extra-legal action in defense of whiteness, capitalism, and the state. These geographies are less likely to have gone through the civil rights revolution that transformed the bureaucracy, police forces, and governance of larger cities. Furthermore, in smaller cities, towns and suburbs, working-class whites are experiencing a collapse of white privilege, often resulting in deaths of despair. This growing immiseration is ripe for recruitment into the far-right, which blames immigrants and urban people of color for the downfall of society. A revolutionary strategy for civil war will have to split the white proletariat in these areas and win over a section of them to a revolutionary program.

Let's not have any illusions about it: the political and demographic divisions that pit cities, towns, suburbs, and the countryside against each other would be profoundly difficult to navigate in a civil war scenario. In this context, a revolutionary movement would have to win over the workers who are in the food and manufacturing industries. Many of these workers are not located in big cities, where people tend to work in retail, service, and logistical sectors, but in smaller cities, towns, suburbs and in the countryside. While these territories tend to be predominantly white, there are a significant number of people of color concentrated in agricultural and manufacturing workforces in these places. The labor force of the large farms where most food is produced in this country, for example, is largely made up of Latinx workers. These workers would be crucial in connecting gentrified cities to a process of socially coordinated production. The revolution cannot succeed by only taking over city squares, condos, bank headquarters, etc.

As the geography of revolutionary struggle spreads beyond major cities, what will link these vast territories together? Will it be organizations, social media, cars, crisis, or the rising tide of mass struggles? It will probably take a combination of all these forces and elements in new and creative ways weaving strong and lengthy threads that cover hundreds of miles. The vast size of this country certainly plays a powerful political role in keeping proletarians separate from one another. Is it possible for militants to use cars and the highway system in order to coordinate and organize the forces of insurrection on a regional and national level?

The Latinx Proletariat

Whereas the first civil war was basically a Black and white affair, the second US civil war would be much more complex. The greatest demographic difference between the first civil war and the second civil war is the growth of the Latinx proletariat. As of today, Latinx people account for 18.5% of the population, and there are more Latinx people in the country than there are Black people. To the extent that Latinx proletarians make up a disproportionate part of the agriculture sector, what they do in a revolutionary crisis will be decisive, since they have the potential to counterbalance the racism of the mostly white countryside. The Latinx proletariat could play a vital role in a revolutionary process, because they are in exactly those industries which will be needed to feed the revolution.

Masses of proletarians from Latin America have migrated to the so-called United States and have become a cheap labor force for American capitalism, working in the lowest paying jobs. They are hunted by ICE (Immigration and Customs Enforcement) and under the constant threat of deportation. The abolitionist framework of the uprising is ripe for resisting ICE and other apparatuses of deportation. Antagonism with ICE has been a feature of the overall uprising. Even before the eruption of the George Floyd uprising, undocumented prisoners were already rebelling against the poor sanitary conditions in ICE detention centers.

Yet, at the same time that they occupy a highly precarious position within the US class structure, Latinx proletarians are simultaneously wooed by whiteness and can display strong anti-Black tendencies. Most immigrants are taught all kinds of anti-Black garbage. Much of the immigrant rights movement and their emphasis on immigrants being good, law abiding, hard workers easily slips into anti-Blackness.

Like all sections of the working class, the Latinx proletariat has many contradictory tendencies. The term "Latinx" is itself a fairly loose and broad term, one which fails to capture the internal dynamics and contradictions of any community that might be defined as such. Divisions of gender, ethnicity, class and nationality result in different political and economic relationships to capital and the state. Another important contradiction is how Latinx US citizens view undocumented immigrants. There is a sizable portion with papers who view undocumented immigrants as criminals who skipped the line. These and other contradictions will have to be worked out in the process of mass revolutionary activity.

While much of our analysis focuses on Black and white relations within the proletariat, it is undeniable that the Latinx proletariat would be a decisive force in a civil war scenario, particularly because so many Latinx workers currently work in some of the most important industries in the country, especially farms and food processing centers. While we are inspired by the fact that a layer of Latinx proletarians participated and fought alongside Black and white proletarians in the 2020 riots, the deepening of this shared struggle is not at all guaranteed. To begin with an assumption that darker skin color automatically translates into political unity is a gross simplification. Nor does shared oppression always mean unity. Like all proletarians, the Latinx proletariat is faced with a choice: join the uprising, abstain from the uprising, or attack the uprising. This choice will inevitably be framed in terms of whiteness, solidarity with Black liberation, citizenship, borders, and work. How the Black movement navigates each of these specific fields of struggle will have a powerful influence on what Latinx proletarians decide to do.

The Social Revolution

How does crisis and civil war impact the development of a revolutionary movement? Does the present escalation of political tensions doom us to become foot-soldiers for different factions of the bourgeoisie? Or can we transform the current crisis into a revolutionary war to overthrow capitalism?

What is the relationship between civil war and revolution? How will things change when tens of millions of people do not have enough income, food to eat, and money for rent?

In the course of its struggle against the ruling class, any revolutionary movement is forced to defend itself against the state and the forces of counter-revolution. Any attempt to challenge power will always be met with repression and violence, which must be countered in order to further intensify and expand the revolutionary struggle. As we can see today and throughout history, the tension between revolution and counter-revolution gives rise to a latent civil war which risks eventually exploding into an open shooting war. The danger of any civil war is that it could decenter the focus of resistance away from the state and capitalism, into the realm of sectarian conflict. In the face of this mounting danger, rather than trying to avoid civil war, we believe that the task of revolutionaries is to engage with these polarizing dynamics in a manner that topples capital and the state while expanding the realm of participation in a social revolution.

Social revolution, while inseparable from the civil war, is its own distinct process. The shape that social revolution takes is determined by the methods by which proletarians fight, their selection of targets, and their political imagination. Concretely, this means smashing commodity relations by taking over the necessary institutions and sites of production and creating a classless system of social reproduction for everyone, in which wealth is no longer indexed to labor time. The social revolution entails not only the mass self-activity of the proletariat in its struggle to take over the infrastructure of society, but also the manner in which it captures people's imagination and wins people over to the end goal it imagines for itself: the overthrow of capitalism. By involving a critical mass of people in the process of taking over society, the social revolution reduces the scope and scale of a potential civil war. In this manner, the fate of the civil war and social revolution are inversely linked.

While the US Civil War entailed a revolt of property (in the shape of Black humans) against the slave power, today the revolutionary subject is a proletariat hunted by police, and facing the grossest inequality in generations, which will have to confront the spectacle of a fully commodified society. That the preamble to what might become the second civil war started with an anti-cop uprising makes sense in a moment where the state's social welfare services have retreated, while its repressive apparatus has ballooned in the last fifty years. At the same time, many participants also came out during the uprising because of the economic effects of the pandemic, their hatred of Donald Trump, and because it gave them a way to finally fight back against this system. These and other grievances were all poured into the container of the George Floyd uprising. The container cannot hold all these issues, and that is why things will continue to explode.

How the container explodes matters. In one version the demands of Black liberation will be forgotten or watered-down—abolishing the police, prisons, and the rest of the carceral apparatus will be sidelined. In the second version all movements carry forth an abolitionist perspective and there is a deepening of the process of social revolution. In this version, abolition is not a set of reforms to defund the police, prisons, and military. Revolutionary abolition is a class war on all portions of society that seek to monitor, discipline, and control proletarian life. Abolition cannot happen without a social revolution that destroys capitalism and the state. This connection is not hard to imagine, as police continue to evict people from homes, protect grocery stores and warehouses from hungry proletarians, and murder Black proletarian and other working-class people. However, the official BLM groups have not grasped this class dynamic at all, and generally try to contain the movement into an ethnic patronage system.

The actual uprising, where strikes, riots, the takeover of buildings, and the creation of autonomous zones occurred—this is the way forward. In this sense, the embryo of revolution already exists in the present, and our task is to connect with it and to engage in direct action that can help it grow in a more strategic direction. Either these struggles will spread into new forms of mass action, or the movement eventually will become isolated and will be defeated. We feel that revolutionaries can play an important role in this process, even if the broader movement will most likely not understand itself in terms of anarchism, socialism, or communism. Instead, it is more likely that a revolutionary movement will see itself as finishing the civil war, under the resurrected banner of abolition.

"We don't have the guns, we're not ready"

The US is the most heavily armed society on earth. This passion for firearms stems from the legacy of settler-colonialism and slavery on which this nation was founded. Today, the majority of guns are not in the hands of people we would consider friends or comrades. This is a difficult fact. On paper, a shootout would result in a quick defeat for our side. But the success of revolutionary movements cannot be tallied by a simple accounting of who has the most guns. If that were the case, the Vietnamese would have never defeated the U.S. military, nor would the slaves in Haiti have stood a chance against Napoleon's army. No dictatorship would have ever been overthrown in history. And yet it is undeniable that these things have happened and continue to happen.

Revolutions are not shootouts between good guys and bad guys. A successful revolution will not come from a vanguard of armed revolutionaries but from millions of everyday people engaging in riots, strikes, occupations, and other forms of mass struggle. We will not all of a sudden buy more guns than the right. Instead, it is the political divisions that the mass movement can cause in society that can radically change the mathematics on guns. This means splitting the white population, yes, but most importantly, it means splitting the National Guard and the armed forces and winning a section of them to the side of the revolution. Not only will these forces have the guns, but they will know how to use them and know how to train others. To this end, we should exploit openings within the rank and file of the military. During the Vietnam war, soldiers—Black soldiers in particular—rebelled against their officers. During the uprising this summer, National Guard units refused orders to attack protesters and instead put down their weapons. Moments like these need to be engaged with and taken seriously by revolutionaries. Building alliances among rank-and-file soldiers can destabilize the repressive power of the state and will be crucial in determining the outcome of a revolutionary conflict.

While taking over the crucial means of production needed to feed, clothe, and care for everyone, it will also be necessary to defend these units of production from the forces of counter-revolution, which of course includes the police, but also a hardcore of racist whites who will defend capitalism to the end. This racist core must be overcome and destroyed in the process of a social revolution that splits the military and splits white society. In this sense there will be a need for guns, but the balance of forces does not rest on who has more guns. On the contrary, the balance of forces will be fundamentally decided by the mass character of our movement, our ability to seize key points of production, and our ability to project the most emancipatory set of politics we can imagine.

Defending the gains of the revolution will require some proletarians to organize as armed groupings. Armed security forces have been a feature of the George Floyd uprising, so this is already happening to an extent. But if these armed groupings become specialized units, they risk instituting a new form of social control, and in the worse-case scenario, they risk becoming a "revolutionary" police force, a "people's army", or a "worker's state." In other words, if the armed struggle becomes a militaristic struggle of one conventional force against another, the insurgents can only succeed by becoming a new kind of state, a new ruling class, a new phase of capitalism, as happened over and over again in most of the revolutions of the 20th century. This would lead to the demise of any revolutionary process.

Conclusion

Revolutions in general are inseparable from civil wars and we see no reason why that will be any different in the future. To run away from the impending civil war is to run towards liberalism and social democracy, i.e., towards white supremacy. We have no illusions that most will balk at what we say, but just like the first civil war, you do not have a choice. The structure of race and class in the United States makes civil war an inevitable aspect of any revolutionary movement. The more aware we are of this phenomenon, the better we can navigate it and connect it to a process of social revolution. At this point, however, it is the far right that is determining the terms of this protracted conflict. A Biden Presidency will not change this fundamental dynamic. Whether or not the left will develop a coherent strategy of escalation of its own is still unclear. Luckily, a full-blown civil war will not happen tomorrow. There is still some time to prepare.

Many will say that civil war isn't on the table because nowhere among the ruling classes do we see a serious faction pushing for this. At the current moment this is correct. The divisions have appeared on the ground first. But this would be no different from the first civil war. It was the self-activity of slaves running away, abolitionists partaking in decisive direct actions, and the broader issue of the expansion of slave territories that drove the dynamic of escalating partisan conflict. Not until late in the game did the respective ruling classes finally accept that the reality of civil war was upon them. In this sense, to seek the roots of the second civil war at the level of the bourgeoisie is a mistake. The seeds of the Second Civil War will grow from the ground upwards, as they did the first time around. In fact, the bourgeoisie will likely be the last class to accept that revolution and civil war are upon us. This is because it has the most to lose.

Our fundamental belief is that for a successful proletarian revolution to take place in the US, the racial order will have to be thoroughly overturned and defeated in the process. It is only by intensifying and deepening such a struggle, which threatens to split all of society, that the contradictions surrounding race will be settled once and for all.

Of course, the dynamic process that tethers revolution to civil war entails very serious dangers—namely, the diverting of social revolution into sectarian conflict, as occurred in Syria in the early 2010s. In accounting for this danger, we have spelled out in broad terms the strategies that may minimize the potential for civil war while expanding the potential for social revolution. Our ideal is a social revolution which has split and won over enough whites and non-Black proletarians to the cause of abolition and reconstruction that the civil war is a minimal aspect of the revolution. While this will happen through street riots, in order for such a movement to succeed in the long run, larger sections of the proletariat will have to develop organized responses to the crisis of capitalism; this will largely depend on the ability to seize, defend, and transform the industries that are necessary for social reproduction. The exact details of how this will be done can only be answered by proletarians acting and thinking on the ground and on their own initiative.

4

Fire on Main Street

Small Cities in the George Floyd Uprising

SHEMON SALAM, ARTURO CASTILLON, AND ATTICUS BAGBY-WILLIAMS

The small city still does not exist on the map of the left as far as revolutionary struggle is concerned. Instead, the revolutionary left in the United States is mostly focused on big cities, resulting in a kind of parochialism where most revolutionaries live in big cities and are more likely to know comrades in other big cities, even overseas in cities like Berlin, Paris or London, but have no relationships with revolutionaries in the small cities and suburbs a few miles outside their city.

In geographic terms, the historical and cultural poles of the revolutionary left milieu in the USA are Oakland and New York City. Most movement texts and organizational strategy come from these two cities. On one level, this limited geography reflects the class background, cultural status, university education, and coastal biases which map onto the liberalism of left-wing activists since the 2008 crisis. For example, Occupy was a national movement with camps scattered throughout the country, but the focus was still on New York and Oakland.

With the 2014 riots in Ferguson, we can now look back and say that this rebellion foreshadowed a wider geography of struggle, although that was not clear at the time. Most people had not heard of Ferguson before the police murder of Mike Brown and the riots that followed. Suddenly a small St. Louis suburb was the center of national attention. While NYC and Oakland were not necessarily displaced as the extreme poles of the revolutionary left, they were no longer in a dance only with each other, but were circling around a new center of gravity—the small suburban city. But as the fires of Ferguson disappeared, the binary emerged once again between NYC and Oakland.

When the George Floyd uprising erupted throughout the United States, dozens of riots happened in smaller cities like Spokane (Washington State), Eugene (Oregon), Fargo (North Dakota), Salt Lake City (Utah), Atlantic City (New Jersey), Lynchburg (Virginia), Columbia (South Carolina), Fort Lauderdale (Florida). The large and midsize cities certainly showed up, with explosive riots in places like Minneapolis, Oakland, Portland, New York City, Philadelphia, Atlanta, Miami. While much attention has been given to these larger cities, the riots in the small cities and suburbs have been largely overlooked. The only exception here is Kenosha, which couldn't be ignored after an armed white counter-protester fired his automatic rifle at BLM protesters and killed two of them.

Riots are growing in small cities and suburbs throughout the country, but this isn't an entirely new phenomenon either. The riots of the 1960s had already exposed a wider geography of struggle, although most people do not remember this era in this way. Alongside big cities like Los Angeles, Chicago, and Detroit, small cities also exploded in places like Rochester (New York State), York (Pennsylvania), Omaha (Nebraska), and even in small towns and suburbs like Wadesboro (North Carolina), Saginaw (Michigan), Plainfield (New Jersey), and Cairo (Illinois). In fact, nearly half of the riots during the "long hot summer" of 1967 happened in small cities and towns.

Perhaps we might remember the riots in smaller cities like Cincinnati in 2001, Benton Harbor in 2003, or Toledo in 2005 differently if other world historical events had not happened in the early 2000s: 9/11, the war on Afghanistan and Iraq, hurricane Katrina in New Orleans, and of course, the 2008 economic crisis. These gigantic events suffocated how we understood the beginning of the 21st century, by drowning out the struggles that were happening against the state. Only now, years later, can we connect the dots from event to event, and see that a process was unfolding which ultimately led to the summer of 2020.

Clearly, it is not large cities alone that set the stage for riots and uprisings. Given the growing suburbanization of where proletarians live and work in the

US, our wager is that small cities and suburbs will increasingly play a role in the battles and ruptures that are coming. Therefore, it's crucial that we analyze the particular dynamics of these places and the strategic implications that they pose.

Class Conflict in the Peripheries

The George Floyd uprising, like the Ferguson riots before it, revealed a growing proletarian stratum which no longer lives in big cities. As small cities and suburbs continue to grow in population, they have also become home to a more diverse cross-section of the proletariat which is increasingly Latinx and Black. This stratum broke through in the 2020 uprising, in smaller cities like San Bernardino (California), Des Moines (Iowa), Champaign (Illinois), Lansing (Michigan), Albany (New York State), Brockton (Massachusetts), Providence (Rhode Island), Richmond (Virginia), Birmingham (Alabama), and elsewhere.

While poor people are still over-represented in the largest cities, poverty has grown in small cities and suburbs for decades now, but especially since the 2008 crisis, which increased the rate of home foreclosures in these areas. At the same time, a growing number of proletarians are leaving the biggest cities as they get more gentrified and become more expensive to live in, instead finding more affordable housing in the suburbs and small cities that surround the big cities. This trend is also reinforced by the fact that working class jobs continue to shift away from the urban core and into the suburbs and small cities on the periphery of the metropolis.

Of course, small cities are not homogenous, and in fact exhibit sharp differences. The small metropolis is very different from the suburb or satellite city, not just in terms of size and population but more importantly in terms of political economy. Whereas small cities like Kenosha or Wauwatosa are suburbs of larger cities like Milwaukee, a small metropolis like Birmingham, Durham, or Albany, forms its own economic core and has its own suburbs.

We can further divide the political economy of small cities into two types. The first type is the left-behind city: this is the small city which has received little to no capital investment, more commonly known as gentrification. This includes small cities like Rockford (Illinois), Chester (Pennsylvania), Forest Park (Georgia), or Kenosha (Wisconsin). Most of the small rust-belt cities in the Northeast and Midwest fall into this first category, although small, immiserated cities are scattered throughout the US.

The second type is the small city which has seen a significant influx of capital investment, cities like Durham (North Carolina), Pittsburgh (Pennsylvania), Lancaster (Pennsylvania), or Rochester (New York State). Here investment is about revitalizing the small city as a tourist destination, and as a hub for white-collar jobs in healthcare, technology and education. Of course, this kind of investment does not mean less racism or less poverty for the proletariat, which still finds itself relegated to low-wage jobs with no benefits and no job security.

As some small cities make their downtown areas more attractive to suburbanites and yuppies, the same pattern plays out as in the big cities—proletarians get priced out of the commercialized urban core and pushed into the peripheries of the city where rent is more affordable. Despite the small shopping districts, art, cultural and entertainment centers, highly concentrated pockets of racialized poverty continue to grow in these small cities, reinforcing the social inequality and racial boundaries that eventually explode into open revolt, as we saw in the Daniel Prude riots in Rochester and in the Ricardo Munoz riot in Lancaster, both in early September.

The Limits of Big Cities

If we take a city like New York City and broaden its geography to the overall NYC metro area, we will quickly see that the city is completely dependent on its surrounding region for survival. Looking at things from this vantage point means we need to ask the following questions: from where and whom do we get our food? Our electricity? Our water? Fuel and replacement parts for subways and buses? And other essential goods we need to survive?

For example, where does NYC get its power? 31% comes from nuclear power, 44% from natural gas, and 19% from hydro power. None of this is produced in New York City itself. Each of these power sources are located somewhere else, and electrical transmission lines have to deliver the power to the city. From the standpoint of power infrastructure, the NYC region stretches hundreds if not thousands of miles. To think of NYC in an isolated way when it comes to power is to fall short in understanding the broader territories, infrastructures, and relations that make a place like NYC possible.

Our point is not to argue that struggles in big cities are useless or anything like that. The radical milieu that exists in larger cities can have a big impact on the political development of revolutionaries in smaller cities, and that cross-pollination is important. However, our argument is that if we are serious about revolution, big cities alone are not enough. Just like socialism in one country was impossible, so is revolution in one big city. This is because big cities are not isolated islands but exist in tight relations with their surrounding geography.

It is worth remembering the experience of the Paris Commune. Here geography was inseparable from the defeat of the revolution. In the course of a proletarian uprising, Paris went hungry because the siege by the bourgeoisie effectively blockaded the city and isolated it from the food producing regions of France. Paris was not exceptional, but a pattern that repeated itself in revolutionary movements across the decades, in Barcelona, Shanghai, Athens, Aleppo. Even with a narrow focus on food in mind, it should be clear that there is no serious possibility of revolution if we cannot find solidarity outside of big cities. Any road to revolution will have to tackle this problem politically and logistically. Otherwise, our fate will be that of the communards: hunger and isolation.

In an era where cities produced massive amounts of industrial goods, James Boggs and Grace Lee Boggs wrote "The City is the Black Man's Land",[1] pointing to the unique position of Black proletarians in core industrial cities in the North. Capturing cities like Baltimore, Newark, or Detroit in the 1960s was not only symbolic, but a real node of material power that could be connected to the Black Revolution. The Republic of New Afrika pointed out a flaw in Boggs' thinking, arguing that Northern cities were surrounded by a sea of white racists. In contrast, it was Southern Black cities, nestled in an ecology of Black rural areas, which could provide the dynamic exchange of resources we have discussed. However, a revolutionary commune of the sort that Paris had in 1871 was never built in the US. Perhaps the closest analogy could be the rise of Black political elites in major cities, but this is a crass analogy. None of these Black mayors did anything radical, but they quickly ran into the same geographic limits of being surrounded by hostile metro and regional areas. They were starved of capital investment and a tax base, and these cities became highly immiserated. If this is what capital can do in these reformist

---

1.   *Monthly Review* 17 (11), April 1966: https://doi.org/10.14452/MR-017-11-1966-04_4

circumstances, imagine what capital will do if cities go all out in an anti-capitalist insurrection!

Our focus on small cities, therefore, is not moralistic, but strategic. Small cities are often important nodes which bridge into rural areas. Unlike midsize and large cities, small cities are surrounded not only by suburbs, but also by exurbs and the countryside, places where agriculture, energy production, and extractive industries are more concentrated. We have not talked about urban economies in terms of metropolitan regions, but small cities and suburbs also constitute a growing part of the metropolitan economy. While manufacturing has largely left the big cities, it has often migrated to suburbs a few miles away. Small cities and suburbs are also a crucial part of the logistical backbone of the US, playing an essential function in the distribution, transportation, and storage of commodities. Amazon and Walmart distribution centers are often found in these places.

For some the lesson of the riots this summer is that we must fight the police. This lesson only makes sense as part of a larger plan that develops coordination between small cities, suburbs, and big cities. Fighting the police is not an end, but a means to an end, and if we are not careful, it can become a dead-end. For us, the crucial lesson of the 2020 uprising concerns the questions of infrastructure, territory, power, and revolution. How does the riot generalize into an insurrection and from there a revolution? For all the reasons listed above, we believe that small cities and suburbs are an essential part of how this happens.

Strategic Particularities

The riots in small cities exhibited some of the same characteristics as those in the big cities. Police departments were quickly overwhelmed by multi-racial crowds that came together to attack the police and sabotage property. While the political counterinsurgency has a smaller base in smaller cities (because of the lack of nonprofits, lack of Democratic Party infrastructure, and the lack of a Black middle-class), counterinsurgency nonetheless still happened in these places, as middle-class activists and local politicians intervened to stop people from rioting and looting.

At the same time, it's important to distinguish what is different about the riots in small cities. The specific environment of these places gives rise to particular forms of struggle: the decentralization of the physical terrain and the centrality of cars allows for greater mobility. In this sense, small cities are fundamentally different from big cities.

Unlike the rigid grid structure of large cities, there is a unique, highly diffuse spatial organization in small cities and towns in which townhouses, apartment buildings, housing complexes and trailer parks are situated in between roads and highways, lawns and estate grounds, patches of woods and parking lots, golf courses and baseball fields, strip malls and shopping centers, all of which make it much more difficult for police to create choke points to corral people and make mass arrests. Thus, there's much more strategic depth available to the movement of the crowd.

Furthermore, unlike the police in New York City, Los Angeles, or other large cities which regularly train in riot tactics, police departments in small cities are generally inept and ill-trained when it comes to dealing with hostile crowds. When reacting to riot situations, they are quickly overwhelmed and outmaneuvered in the streets. Rioters and experienced militants can take advantage of this.

Of course, there are also clear disadvantages to insurrection in small cities. Often there are no downtown shopping districts to mobilize around, and when there are, they are very small and easily surrounded. Because there is less concentration of capital in small cities, power is more dispersed and harder to find. Another main disadvantage posed by the small size of these places is that the security state might be more likely to know who key militants are.

Something else that stands out in small cities is the absence of a revolutionary left milieu. This was not always the case, but it has been this way for some time now. This is not meant to insult or look down upon revolutionaries in small cities. In fact, the lack of a leftist milieu might be a blessing in disguise, since there are fewer activists, nonprofit professionals, and academics to mediate, co-opt, or stop the riot.

Because of their unique conditions, militant organizing in these places will look different from big cities. Some radical projects have been happening in places like Mississippi, Indiana, and upstate New York, where revolutionaries are not necessarily protesting all the time or writing articles for a chic radical publication. Instead, they are building spaces, providing resources, rooting themselves in communities and workplaces, and using these activities as a basis to start new conversations about revolt and insurrection.

At the same time, critiques of mutual aid apply in small cities as well. We do not want to be a radical version of the Salvation Army. Nor do we want to reproduce the same narrow political milieu that exists in big cities, but in a smaller form. Our spaces should be places for proletarians to gather, learn, and strategize, and should provide infrastructure that aids in class combat. This requires following and participating in the struggles of the proletariat, which can manifest themselves as workplace militancy, tenant strikes, eviction defense, riots, looting, etc. There is no recipe for this. It has to be carefully developed from the tactical and strategic needs that are organic to each specific struggle.

Building a Bridge Between Small Cities and Big Cities

Revolutionaries in small cities often travel to big cities to take part in demonstrations and support radical organizing, but we are much less likely to see the reverse happen. Rockford, for example, is 90 minutes away from Chicago, but few Chicago based radicals have ever stepped foot in Rockford. Yet proletarians in this small rust-belt city rioted and looted for two nights during the George Floyd uprising this summer. While the Chicago revolutionary left might take part in a nearby rebellion in Kenosha, will their support ever extend beyond that?

This is not a moral argument about breaking out of our bubble, but a direct and immediate problem about how we will survive the capitalist crisis and reproduce our ability to live and fight. From the standpoint of revolutionary strategy, making connections to small cities is a key part of preventing the isolation of big cities, which are entirely dependent on the ecology of their surrounding regions. If the goal is revolution, it is imperative that militants in big cities begin to build trusting relationships with militants in these smaller peripheral cities. Instead of taking a dozen flights to Oakland or New York City, Berlin or Paris, a serious orientation towards revolution in the United States will involve driving hours outside of Oakland or New York City and building political relationships with people in small cities like Vallejo, Manteca, Modesto and Merced, or Allentown, Scranton and Utica.

This will be very difficult to do. For starters, while jobs are increasingly shifting to smaller cities and suburbs, it is still true that most jobs concentrate in large urban cores, and even revolutionaries need to hold down jobs under capitalism. But there are other intangible limitations that will also make it hard. Small cities are places of isolation, devoid of big museums, famous music venues, and other interesting cultural forms that we enjoy in big cities. And to the extent that we travel to try to meet comrades who are similar to ourselves, we might find no one on the other side of this trip. This creates many problems with no easy solutions. The current demarcations and constitution of the ultra-left makes meeting our other half very difficult. Niche texts and authors only become common knowledge among the dense ecology of revolutionaries that live in big cities. In small cities this is much less likely. Instead of beginning from a textual starting point, it makes more sense to start from the tasks, tactics, strategy, and political horizons that have emerged out of the George Floyd uprising. The basis for these possibilities is the generalized crisis which the pandemic, capitalism, and the uprising have generated.

Conclusions

There are several interrelated conclusions. First, we believe that some revolutionaries should move to these smaller peripheral cities and connect with proletarian militants in these places, as they are closer to food, manufacturing, logistical, and power infrastructures. Second, even if we do not move to these smaller cities, we still need to develop real political relationships with the militants in these places. Third, we need to learn as much from revolutionaries in small cities as we do from revolutionaries in big cities. Fourth, we need to abandon our big city-centric approach to organizing and develop a new praxis that wrestles with the complex geography of class conflict.

It is the logistics of revolution that should set the basis for how we organize, where we organize, and who we organize with. Only by basing our strategies and horizons in that vantage point does our argument make sense. We look to new geographies which do not center finance or real estate capital, the university, or the tiny milieu of the radical left, but instead search for what is required to make revolution a real possibility, and that means seeing the world differently. It has not been any text that has made this perspective possible, but the revolts of the George Floyd uprising. We are merely scribes of the uprising, trying to connect the riots and street fighting to the real possibility of insurrection and revolution. We do not see the riots as simply riots, but as a process of struggle that opens up the possibility for the overthrow of capitalism. This path closes along the current trajectory of the big city-centric left, which is literally the left-wing of capital in its material position. Instead of a left that converges in big cities, we need a left rooted in the expansive geography of critical infrastructure and proletarian life.

In light of the history of this country, our argument is not so far-fetched. The dynamic relationship between the urban center and the periphery has been a feature of many radical struggles here: the Maroon communities, the Underground Railroad, Industrial Workers of the World, Congress of Industrial Organizations, and the Student Nonviolent Coordinating Committee. Even today the proletariat has connected some of the dots. It is us, in the radical left who are trailing behind them, trying to catch up, and often in the way of their advance. While the proletariat has not completed the map, it has shown us some important paths and directions we must take.

We know that infrastructure is key in sustaining capitalist flows, but what does this infrastructure mean in the context of an insurrection? Blockading infrastructure like airports or highways makes sense at times. But how long can you hold a blockade if your city runs out of food? What happens when you need clean, running water? What happens when you need electricity? Is the goal to blockade power facilities or to take them over? How do we prevent the political and ultimately military isolation of large cities?

This summer's riots have yet to propose an alternative. In this sense they are critiques of racial capitalism and the police, but as soon as the riots become conscious of themselves, they will have to propose an alternative to capitalism. We must do everything in our power so that the coming riots transform into insurrections, so that the flag of the commune-maroon community is raised once again, and where all the questions of geography, of who, where, and what, will be front and center. It is these questions which revolutionaries need to start thinking about and trying to answer, not only theoretically, but in practice. This means spending some serious time and energy rooting ourselves in small cities.

Protesters around the White house to demand justice over George Floyd's death. Washington DC, on May 30, 2020.

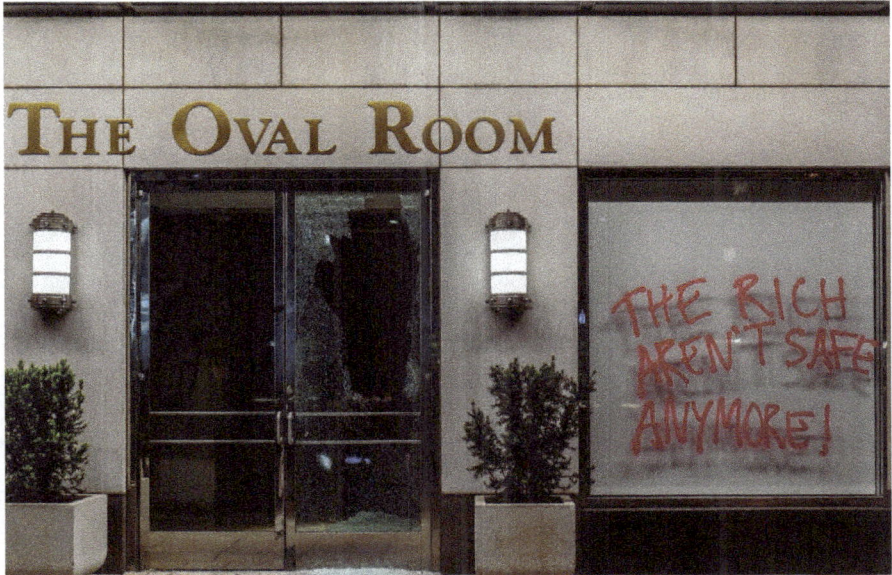

Protesters gathered around the White house to demand justice over George Floyd's death. Washington DC, USA on May 31, 2020

5

Postscript on the 2020 Riots

SHEMON SALAM AND ARTURO CASTILLON

If the summer belonged to Black liberation and riots, the winter has shifted in favor of a reactionary right-wing offensive. In the aftermath of the George Floyd uprising, Trump's claim that the Democrats stole the election resulted in a mob of right-wingers storming the US capitol on January 6th. But if the horizon of the 2020 uprising was a common attack on racism and class inequality, then the horizon of January 6th was about restoring the declining power of the middle-class, especially the white middle-class. It should come as no surprise that the forces that stormed the Capitol made up the same demographic that organized the paramilitary repression of the 2020 riots: a mostly white petit bourgeoisie, and in particular, small business owners.[1]

As we discussed in "The Return of John Brown: White Race Traitors in the 2020 Uprising",[2] whites who joined the Black led rebellions were countered by reactionary whites who wanted to enforce the boundaries of racial capitalism. This conflict between whites often exploded into open violence during the 2020 riots. This violence reached a climax in August in Kenosha (Wisconsin), where several young white people who joined the uprising there were shot and murdered by a white gunman acting under the guise of protecting small

---

1. Lambert Strether (January 20, 2021) "The class composition of the Capitol rioters (First Cut)", *MR Online*.

2. Shemon and Arturo (September 4, 2020) The Return of John Brown: The Rise of Race Traitors in the 2020 Uprising, *Ill Will Editions*.

businesses and private property from looters. Here we see how class plays a fundamental role in shaping and enforcing whiteness. This enforcement is not unique to the far-right, but is the general task of all middle-class whites.

It's important to remember the middle-class nature of January 6th and of the broader right-wing offensive, because in the United States, it is easy to slip into losing a class analysis of whites. If we forget that just months earlier white proletarians were fighting alongside Black proletarians, we will make catastrophic political, strategic, and ethical mistakes.

The conflict among whites reflects the broader dynamic of civil war that continues to engulf all of society. This is not to say that we are literally in a civil war today, but that the splitting of society along partisan lines is one of the preconditions of civil war. In the United States, civil war is the medium through which the race question is settled, and so, another inflection point was reached on January 6th. But to fully understand January 6th we have to return to the fires of the George Floyd uprising.

The last proletarian assault of 2020 was in October in Philadelphia, in response to the police murder of Walter Wallace Jr. No doubt, liberals worried that the Philadelphia rebellion would cost them the election in Pennsylvania (a swing state) and would justify a law-and-order counter-attack by Republicans. Yet the Black proletarians who rioted in Philly could not have cared less. Justice for Walter Wallace Jr. was not in the voting booth, but in the streets.

The week of November 4th saw open air celebrations break out across the country as Biden won the election. Many felt that they had defeated fascism, but a few Black activists were already going on twitter to remind everyone that Mike Brown, Eric Garner, and Korryn Gaines were all murdered under the presidency of a Democrat, Barack Obama. Although liberals promised that Biden would return America back to normal, things only escalated when Trump wouldn't concede the election. This created the general conditions which led to January 6th. But before we jump into that, we want to look at two previous conflicts that involved the Proud Boys and other Trump loyalists in Washington DC, on November 14th and December 12th. The lack of proletarians among Antifa and BLM during these large street battles was devastating for the left. Overall, the Proud Boys and their far-right allies were tougher, bigger, and willing to commit considerably more violence than Antifa or BLM.

The proletariat was for the most part not interested in defending Biden and so-called US democracy, let alone the Capitol Building, against the far-right, and instead abstained from the street clashes, letting Antifa/BLM and the Proud Boys battle it out. Still, it was noticeable that the far-right made no attempt to march through proletarian neighborhoods in DC, instead sticking to the downtown area. Given that multiple Proud Boys and Trump supporters got stabbed in DC during a prior conflict with Black proletarians on November 4th, there is a sense that if the far-right had marched on Black working class neighborhoods in DC, they would not have come out alive. This estimation gives us some hope.

January 6th was certainly not successful in accomplishing a seizure of power, yet it was a profound leap by the far-right which must go down as a historic event. It is reasonable to expect January 6th to shape the political terrain in the near future. We already see it on two counts. The first is that the law-and-order practice of the state is on full display: the FBI on a nationwide manhunt for protestors who entered the Capitol Building on the 6th, and 25,000 or more National Guards deployed to DC for Biden's inauguration. The second way that the political terrain has shifted is the cowardly and nationalistic posturing of the Democratic Party and the liberals. The same people who were chanting Black Lives Matter last summer during the uprising, were now rallying for law and order to put down the insurgent far-right—the same law and order that proletarians had rebelled against just months before! For much of the left, the Capitol Building suddenly became the sacred ground of US democracy, which now had to be defended against a supposedly treasonous Trump. This is the same Capitol Building where bailouts to corporations, backroom deals, and funding for US imperialism happens. This might be holy ground for the bourgeoisie, but for the proletariat, the Capitol Building is nothing less than the Death Star.

The tragedy of January 6th wasn't that the US Capitol was taken over, its windows smashed, and a cop beaten to death. The tragedy is that it wasn't the mass power of the proletariat that accomplished this. In such a scenario, where the momentum of the George Floyd uprising has come to an end, the danger posed by an increasingly insurgent far-right becomes even more pressing. Calling on the police to criminalize the far-right will only strengthen the police-state, the enemy of the proletariat. So, the question arises: How do we defeat the Proud Boys and other far-right militants of this sort, who are so dedicated to upholding capitalism, prisons, police, and the border, to the point that they are attempting to wage an insurgency?

The middle-class obsession with shouting at enemies, even willingly taking a beating in order to gain the moral high ground, doesn't work with the police, and it certainly doesn't work when confronting the far-right. The proletariat knows this. Still, violence is never off the table when confronting racists and fascists. The proletariat also knows this. An example that we can turn to is the Toledo rebellion of 2005, where after fighting Neo-Nazis in the street, Black proletarians began rioting and looting. The podcast, *It Did Happen Here*,[3] which documents the radical history of anti-racist militants in Portland and Minneapolis in the 1980s and 1990s, also highlights other important examples.

If we are to defeat the right-wing forces that mounted this offensive, then they must be confronted by the collective violence of the proletariat, not the state or law and order. The idea that the proletariat can fight the far-right might seem laughable to some, considering that they currently outgun most of us. But as the summer of 2020 showed us, we do not know what the proletariat is capable of until it actually fights. While we risk overstatement, it might be more accurate to say that when the proletariat unleashes its full power, it cannot be stopped. But too many forces conspire to keep the proletariat in its place, so we rarely get the chance to see what our power actually looks like. In 2020, we got a glimpse of it.

It is not clear now if we are merely carrying the flame of the George Floyd uprising as historians, or if we are strategists preparing for a new round of struggle in the immediate future. The COVID-19 pandemic, the far-right, the economic crisis, and the crisis of the state are all beating down on the proletariat, and we expect little to change in the near future. During the winter we saw the terrain shift to electoralism, from cities to capitals, while the middle-class re-asserted itself not only through the far-right, but also through BLM and mainstream left politics. The geography, composition, and tactics of struggle all shifted away from the proletariat. This is to be expected. As in sports, each team switches back and forth between offense and defense. So too in the class struggle, the proletariat and bourgeoisie alternate between offense and defense. The summer was the offensive of the proletariat, while the winter became more about surviving the attacks of the state and the far-right. As the

---

3. itdidhappenherepodcast.com

pandemic, racist policing, and the crisis of US capitalism continue to deepen, we expect to see a new offensive of the proletariat sooner or later.

While Trump isn't the president anymore, the USA is clearly still in a stage of decline and crisis. We are at the beginning of very hard times, not the end. The Democrats cannot resolve this crisis, nor can they extinguish the spirit of revolt that has gripped much of the proletariat. However, what the future will bring is somewhat unclear. All we can do here is outline the terrain from which insurgent struggles will likely continue to emerge, the most obvious being the conflict between Black proletarians and the police, who will not stop killing Black people, and will likely want revenge for the 2020 riots. Sadly, it wouldn't be surprising if police violence actually increases. This could easily set off a new round of riots. At the same time, it is probable that the forces of law-and-order will be much more militarily and politically prepared for more uprisings in the future. Nonetheless, the uprising has produced a new generation of militants who now have practical experience in the tactics of class combat. In the face of ongoing crises and inequalities, it is unlikely that they will just sit back and accept their fate.

At the same time, Biden-Harris and the Democratic Party could forestall a new uprising by signaling their willingness to deficit-spend and create reforms. This is not because they are better than the Republicans, but because their approach to managing the system is different and their strategy for preventing revolution is different. Of course, given the crisis of U.S. capitalism, it is unclear whether structural reforms around inequality are actually possible. The biggest indices would be wage increases, affordable housing, and taxing the rich. It appears that a 15-dollar minimum wage may happen, but no one knows what to do about rent and housing other than extending the eviction moratoriums, and increasing taxes on the rich seems out of the question for now. As the USA continues its slow descent into an ever-deepening crisis, the prospects of reform and social democracy only becomes less viable.

If our horizon is a world where no one is ever killed by police, then revolutionary abolition becomes the means, and a world where the state, capitalism, and racialism have been smashed is where we must sail towards. This can only be accomplished by proletarians themselves, through the power they are able to solidify as a class against the bourgeoisie. This is an entirely different calculus from voting and law making. To enter this domain is to enter what we consider the Black Radical Tradition, but this also entails risk, even the potential for incarceration, exile, and death, because at the end of the day, the tradition itself is illegal and dangerous, through and through.

If a new round of struggles will emerge, it will have to answer the questions raised during last summer's uprising: Will we riot for Black women? Will we riot for non-Black people? Will the riots generalize? How do we transform the dynamic of civil war into a proletarian revolution? How can the riots become insurrections and revolutionary communes?

Our ability to smash the far-right and overthrow capitalism depends on the ability of the proletariat to materialize the answers to these questions.

We do not idealize the 2020 riots: our texts have pointed out the strategic, tactical, ethical, and political mistakes that were made. A movement made up almost entirely of young people will certainly make mistakes and our critiques come from a place of complete solidarity and support. We only want the struggles to become more: more anti-capitalist, more anti-state, more anti-racist, more anti-imperialist, more feminist, more queer, more environmentalist, and so on. After a summer of riots, the role of revolutionaries could not be clearer: to expand the revolutionary potential of the proletariat, while opposing the counter-revolutionary tendencies that hold it back.

We do not expect most of the middle-class left to figure out how to do this. Instead, it is the proletariat which will have to chart the course of revolution, and we expect it will be very violent, illegal, and will ultimately make the 2020 riots seem like a polite dance party. But we have faith in the proletarian monster. We only hope that when it returns, we are better prepared.

George Floyd memorial

Minneapolis, Minnesota / USA – May 29 2020: George Floyd memorial honoring black lives matter in Minneapolis riots.

About the authors

Shemon Salam is a communist and anarchist in New York. He has been involved in struggle since 9/11.

Arturo Castillon is an insurrectionary communist living in the NYC-Philadelphia area.

Atticus Bagby-Williams is an anarchist and insurrectionary living in the settler colony known as the United States. Atticus is primarily concerned with radical organizing in small cities and suburbs, black anarchist thought, and revolutionary abolitionism.

www.ingramcontent.com/pod-product-compliance
Lightning Source LLC
Chambersburg PA
CBHW071236290326
41931CB00038B/3214